Speaking Up for Ourselves and Others

Anti-Bias Learning: Social Justice in Action

By Adrienne van der Valk

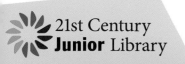
21st Century
Junior Library

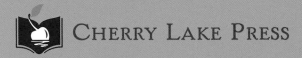

CHERRY LAKE PRESS

Published in the United States of America by Cherry Lake Publishing Group
Ann Arbor, Michigan
www.cherrylakepublishing.com

Developed with help from Learning for Justice, a project of the Southern Poverty Law Center. With special
   thanks to Monita Bell and Hoyt Phillips.
Reading Adviser: Beth Walker Gambro, MS, Ed., Reading Consultant, Yorkville, IL

Photo Credits: © Tom Wang/Shutterstock.com, cover, 1; © Untitled Title/Shutterstock.com, 4; © Bela Zamsha/
   Shutterstock.com, 6; © Matthew Carreiro/ Shutterstock.com, 8; © Diego Cervo/Shutterstock.com, 10;
   © Lopolo/Shutterstock.com, 12; © RobynCharnley/Shutterstock.com, 14; © Sergey Uryadnikov/Shutterstock.
   com, 16; © Atstock Productions/Shutterstock.com, 18; © Monkey Business Images/Shutterstock.com, 20

Cherry Lake Press is an imprint of Cherry Lake Publishing Group.

Library of Congress Cataloging-in-Publication Data has been filed and is available at catalog.loc.gov

Cherry Lake Publishing Group would like to acknowledge the work of the Partnership for 21st Century Learning,
a Network of Battelle for Kids. Please visit http://www.battelleforkids.org/networks/p21 for more information.

Printed in the United States of America
Corporate Graphics

Thank you to Evelyn Anne Marie for advising me during the development of this manuscript.

CONTENTS

5   What Is an Activist?

7   Aspen Is an Activist

13   Rashad Is an Activist

19   YOU Can Be an Activist

22   Glossary

23   Find Out More

24   Index

24   About the Author

You might think of large protest marches when you hear the word "activist," but that's not the only way to make change.

What Is an Activist?

Say the word "**activist**" out loud. Notice that the first sound is the word "act." This is an important clue! An activist is someone who takes action to make a change.

You don't have to be a special kind of person to be an activist. Anyone who is willing to speak up for themselves and others can be an activist.

Think!

How could you learn about activists in your community?

Aspen takes a bus to school. What other ways are there to get to school?

Aspen Is an Activist

Did you know that kids can be activists? It's true!

Meet Aspen. She rides the city bus every morning because she lives in a neighborhood far from her school. Sometimes, the bus is late, and Aspen gets a **tardy** check mark next to her name. Every time she gets three check marks, she has to stay in for recess!

Aspen felt really bad about missing recess. She decided to speak up. She went to her teacher, Mr. Vasquez. She told him she didn't think the rule was fair.

What are some reasons a bus might be running late? Whose fault is it?

"I want to be on time," she told him. "But sometimes, the bus is late, and there's nothing I can do about it."

"Aspen," said Mr. Vasquez. "Why don't you have your parents drive you to school?"

"I don't live with my parents, Mr. Vasquez," said Aspen. "I live with my grandmother, and she goes to work at 5:00 a.m."

"Why don't you take an earlier bus?" said Mr. Vasquez.

"I walk my little sister to day care every morning," Aspen explained. "And she can't be there before 7:30, so I can't catch the earlier bus."

Mr. Vasquez thought about what Aspen said.

Talking with a teacher is a great way to be sure your voice is being heard—even if it feels scary.

"You're right," he said, "That rule is not fair. From now on, I will ask my students why they are late. Thank you, Aspen, for teaching me something today!"

Aspen used her voice to say, "Kids shouldn't be punished for things that aren't their fault."

Make a Guess!

Why do you think Aspen might have felt scared to talk to her teacher?

What are the things you care about?
Rashad cares about animals and their well-being.

Rashad Is an Activist

Meet Rashad. He loves animals. Rashad especially loved one of the cats in his neighborhood. He called her Pounce because she was so playful.

One day, Rashad noticed that Pounce was **limping**. He was worried, so he asked his mother what he could do.

"Pounce is a **stray** cat, and living on the street can be dangerous," his mother said. "The best thing we can do is take Pounce to the **veterinarian** so they can check her leg and **spay** her."

Making cookies for a bake sale is a great way to raise money for an important cause. What else could you do to raise money?

Rashad wanted to help Pounce, but he knew he couldn't do it alone. He decided to talk to his friends Trevor and Carlos. They loved animals too. The three boys spent all afternoon creating their plan.

The next day, Rashad, Trevor, and Carlos set up a table in Rashad's front yard. When the neighbors walked by, they saw the table was filled with boxes of beautiful cookies. Each box had a hand-drawn picture of Pounce on it.

"We're raising money to help Pounce!" the boys explained as people began to crowd around the table.

"Look how cute she is!" one neighbor exclaimed. "I'll take two boxes." People loved the cookies and the pictures of Pounce. Soon, all the cookies were gone!

What other animal causes do you know about?
Ask an adult about what dangers face wild animals.

For the next two weekends, Rashad, Trevor, and Carlos baked cookies and drew pictures. Soon, they had enough money to take Pounce to the vet! They also found her a good home. The boys decided to keep selling cookies so they could help more stray cats in their neighborhood. They used their **talents** and their **creativity** to say, "Animals **deserve** to have good lives."

Create!

Think about something you would like to change. Then write a letter to someone who could help make that change.

Speaking up for what's right doesn't have to be loud.
Sometimes, a quiet conversation makes the biggest change.

YOU Can Be an Activist

You can be an activist like Aspen and Rashad just by speaking up in your own life.

What are some words you can use to speak up for yourself and others? You could say, "I don't think this is right." You could say, "This isn't fair." You could ask, "Why are things this way? How can I make them different?"

Speaking up for yourself and others might feel scary. Aspen probably felt scared to talk to Mr. Vasquez.

We're always stronger when we work together.